D0465343

BipQuiz

100 QUESTIONS & ANSWERS

Weather & Seasons

BipQuiz

100 QUESTIONS & ANSWERS

Weather & Seasons

Illustrations by Florence MacKenzie

Sterling Publishing Co., Inc. New York

10 9 8 7 6 5 4
Published by Sterling Publishing Company, Inc.
387 Park Avenue South, New York, N.Y. 10016
© 1994 by InfoMedia Communication
English translation © 1994 by Sterling Publishing Co., Inc.
Distributed in Canada by Sterling Publishing
% Canadian Manda Group, P.O. Box 920, Station U
Toronto, Ontario, Canada M8Z 5P9
Printed in France - Publiphotoffset, 93500 Pantin
Sterling ISBN 0-8069-0935-8

How to Use the BipPen

The BipPen must be held straight to point to the black dot.

Point to a black dot.

●

A continuous sound (beeeep) and a red light mean that you've chosen the wrong answer.

Point to a black dot.

●

A discontinuous sound (beep beep beep) and a green light mean that you've chosen the right answer.

Keep your BipPen for our other books.

Headings

Each question belongs to a specific heading.
Each heading is identified by a color.

Meteorology

Seasons

Climates

Scientific Data

Various

1

M an has always tried to predict weather according to nature's signs (color of the sky, animals' behavior). Weather science is known as:

meteorology
symphony
speleology

2

E xcept for berries, temperate-region fruits generally ripen in the fall. This is true of the grape, which is used to make wine. Collecting ripe grapes is called:

fertilizing
harvesting
sowing

If it's summer in the Northern Hemisphere, it's winter in the Southern Hemisphere. The demarcation line between the two hemispheres is known as the:

Tropic •
Equator ■
Time Zone ▲

Since the earth is tilted towards the sun, it doesn't receive all of the sun's rays at the same intensity everywhere on the globe. At the Equator, it's always:

hot •
cold ■
freezing ▲

T he earth is surrounded by a layer of air
    that allows for life, and where all
weather happens. This layer is called:

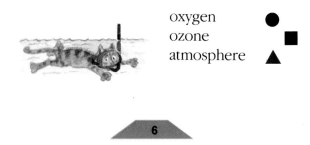

oxygen   ●
ozone   ■
atmosphere   ▲

T emperature decreases as altitude rises,
    which is why some snow never melts,
even during the summer. A river of such ice
is called:

glacial   ●
resistant   ■
melting   ▲

A tmospheric pressure depends on weather and altitude. The higher in altitude one goes, the lower the pressure. Meteorologists measure this pressure with an instrument called:

a barometer

a thermometer

an altimeter

T he cricket is a small insect that "sings" by rubbing its legs and their pointy tips against its wings. It sings louder when:

it becomes warmer

it becomes colder

it starts to rain

S ome clouds give rise to storms. The air, vapor, and ice crystals they contain collide against each other and cause electricity, which appears as:

hail
lightning
thunder

S ome animals come out of hiding after a rainfall. What slow-moving little animal can be found in wet grass?

frog
grasshopper
snail

The first thermometer, invented around 1600 by Galileo, was filled with water. Fahrenheit was the first to systematically use a thermometer containing:

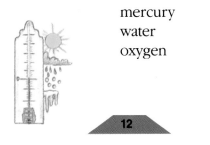

mercury ●

water ■

oxygen ▲

A barometer helps predict weather by measuring air pressure. The higher the pressure, the higher the mercury rises. This means that:

it will rain ●

there will be a storm ■

the weather will be ▲
nice

13

P inecones are very sensitive to humidity. Their scales open up when it is:

dry ●
humid ■
stormy ▲

14

A rainbow always has seven colors, although these colors may vary in intensity. The colors are: red, orange, yellow, green, blue, indigo, and:

black ●
violet ■
brown ▲

I n nice weather, the sky is blue, sometimes with small, distinctly shaped white clouds, which means that air pressure is:

low
high

B uoys are used at sea to measure winds and temperatures in order to help seamen and fishermen. How long have they been used?

1000 years
100 years
30 years

S ince rainbows are rare and beautiful, some civilizations believe that they have magical powers. In Asia, the rainbow is used as a staircase by a deity descending from the sky. This deity's name is:

Buddha ●
Moses ■
Mohammed ▲

E ach cloud carries tons of water vapor, mostly from the sea. This water vapor turns into rain when the droplets that form it become:

heavier
lighter
fewer

C louds are formed when hot and cold air come into contact; clouds also release rain. When it freezes, rain turns into:

snow
lightning
hail

The droplets that constitute rain are so small it takes nearly a million of them to form a single raindrop. The diameter of an average raindrop is about:

10 cm (4″)   ●
1 mm (½₂₇″)   ■
10 mm (⅜″)   ▲

There are ten types of cloud classified according to their shape and height in the sky. One of the most easily recognized, which is white and well defined, is:

the nymph   ●
the cumulus   ■
the diapharous   ▲

S unlight passes through thin clouds, while thicker clouds absorb it, which is why such thick clouds look:

red
white
black

M eteorology is necessary to help fly a plane, to estimate the trip's length and the amount of fuel needed. Predictions can be up to 95% accurate:

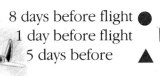

8 days before flight ●
1 day before flight ■
5 days before ▲

S unlight can be of different colors, depending on whether it is diffused by the atmosphere or filtered by a layer of clouds. A red sunset means it will be nice the next day because:

there are no clouds
there are many clouds
you can't see the moon

P rolonged heavy rains or snowmelt can raise the water level of rivers, which can then overflow. What are these overflows called?

floods
baths
seas

Air becomes humid when it absorbs evaporating water. When humidity is high, there is mist. What is the name of a thick mist that keeps visibility low?

fog
clouds
dew

Most countries celebrate their new year in the winter. The Chinese celebrate theirs between January 21 and February 19. For parades, they use fabric and paper to make:

snakes
dragons
lambs

Lightning is caused by the electrical discharges that accompany storms. Only a small part of such lightning falls to the ground, where it can cause extensive damage. This phenomenon is called:

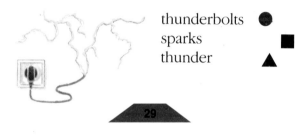

thunderbolts ●

sparks ■

thunder ▲

Spring is a busy time for farmers. The snow has melted, the earth is plowed, and seeds are sown. To enrich the earth, manure or what else is spread?

pesticides ●

vitamins ■

fertilizer ▲

When clouds are thick and heavy, they can produce very heavy rain. What is the name of a very sudden, violent, but brief rainfall?

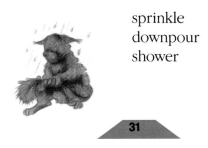

sprinkle ●

downpour ■

shower ▲

Frost forms when water vapor comes into contact with a very cold surfce. Frost can be found in the winter on windows or tree branches. What color is frost?

green ●

white ■

grey ▲

I t measures the amount of water fallen in a single place and is composed of a funnel, which receives water, and a cylindrical tube that measures that water. It is called a:

water meter ●

rain gauge ■

aquameter ▲

A n atmospheric depression means that air pressure is low, and the weather is bad. What does the barometer's needle do under such conditions?

it goes down ●

it goes up ■

it remains immobile ▲

An anticyclone is the opposite of a depression. Winds are mild and the weather is hot and sunny in the summer, cold and sunny in the winter. In western Europe the most frequent anticyclone is from:

the Canary Islands ●

the Azores ■

radars ▲

In 1752, Benjamin Franklin discovered that lightning bolts were electrical phenomena. He invented a long and thin instrument that protects buildings from lightning by directing electricity into the ground:

the lightning rod ●

the weather vane ■

the umbrella ▲

Lightning is dangerous since it conducts electricity. Lightning could strike houses, trees, and people. Where should one never hide during a thunderstorm?

in a car ●
in a house ■
under a tree ▲

For farmers, summer is harvest season. The crops are ripe, ready to be cut or gathered. In temperate regions, the first crops are grains and

strawberries ●
plums ■
apples ▲

When clouds are very cold, lumps of icy rain fall; this is hail. North America has the strongest hailstorms and biggest hailstones. These hailstones can be as big as:

a fingernail ●
a football ■
a fist ▲

The air must be cold in order for it to snow. In countries where it snows a great deal, the words to describe snow are very numerous. The Inuit have how many words to describe snow?

three ●

more than thirty ■

more than one ▲
thousand

Several holidays are observed in winter. Their festivities help relieve the season's rigors. One of these holidays, celebrated by parades of costumed revelers is:

Groundhog Day ●

Arbor Day ■

Mardi Gras ▲

In high altitudes, snow may accumulate on a sheet of ice and slide in a quick and heavy mass towards a valley. This phenomenon is called:

an avalanche ●
a landslide ■
an earthquake ▲

Windmills use the wind's strength to turn their vanes, thus giving necessary energy to the millstone. The vanes are in which position relative to the winds?

behind ●
on the side ■
facing ▲

Hurricanes are strong (over 175 mph [300 km]) winds which can devastate the countryside and can overturn houses. Hurricanes in the Pacific are called:

typhoons
tryphoons
tritons

Tornadoes are damaging winds that spin and turn. They can carry away cars, animals, and pieces of houses with them. Tornado winds are shaped like:

a square
an oval
a funnel

U nlike mountains, oceans offer no resistance to wind, which is why wind often blows so strongly on the beach. The strength of the wind also affects:

the tide
wave height
the presence of rocks

T he simultaneous presence of sun and rain can lead to rainbows. Solar light is reflected in the raindrops and separates into:

seven colours
five colours
ten colours

With the coming of spring, cows and sheep are sometimes taken to the mountains to graze on the new grass. They stay there until the cold weather returns. This migration is called:

alpine season ●

transhumance ■

emigration ▲

In the Bible, the rainbow appears above Noah's Ark after the Flood. The rainbow signals peace between God and man. Thunder, on the other hand, in some ancient religions signified:

the gods' music ●

the gods' cough ■

the gods' wrath ▲

Temperature is measured by some people in degrees Celsius. This system was devised by Celsius, a Swedish astronomer, in 1740. Water boils at 100 degrees, and at 0 degrees, water:

is tepid

freezes

turns to steam

In many countries, the Fahrenheit system is used to measure temperature. What is its symbol?

°F

°Ft

$

There are three great climatic zones on earth: the polar zone, the temperate zone, and the torrid zone. To which zone does North America belong?

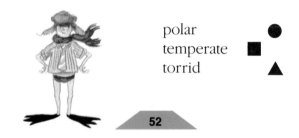

polar ●

temperate ■

torrid ▲

The temperate zone includes oceanic, continental, and Mediterranean climates. The torrid zone includes these climates: equatorial, tropical, and:

humid ●

arid ■

misty ▲

At the northern and southern extremes of the globe, the vast areas of the Arctic and Antarctic are permanently covered by a thick layer of ice that never melts. These regions are called:

glacial
Inuit
polar

In the tropics, there can be 3 or 4 harvests per year, while there can be only two (spring and autumn) in temperate regions. When a farmer decides to let his land rest, it is called:

lying fallow
abandoned
slash and burn

I cebergs are large blocks of ice that break free of glaciers and then float in the sea. Ships must be careful not to hit them. The part of an iceberg underwater accounts for what part of its mass?

⅕ ●

⅖ ■

⅘ ▲

There are four seasons in temperate regions (spring, summer, autumn, and winter). In tropical areas there are two, the wet and dry seasons. Which of the following countries has a tropical climate?

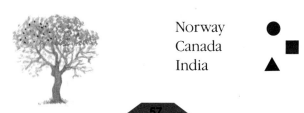

Norway ●
Canada ■
India ▲

Man has always divided the year into seasons. Arabs only recognize three of them: summer, spring, and winter. Autumn was added by which civilization?

Greek ●
Roman ■
Egyptian ▲

E ach season lasts three months. Winter and summer begin with the solstices (days with the shortest and longest duration of daylight of the year). Spring and fall begin with the equinoxes (equal length of day and night). On what day does summer begin in the Northern Hemisphere?

May 21 ●

June 21 ■

June 30 ▲

E ach season has its own characteristics. What reminds you most of autumn?

deep snow ●

ice storms ■

colorful leaves ▲

S ome animals eat all through the fall and spend winter sleeping in a warm place while waiting for spring. This is called:

hibernating
accommodating
pampering

T he tropical climate, with its heat and rain, encourages the development of abundant vegetation and dense forests. The world's largest tropical forest is:

the Amazon forest
the Yellowstone forest
Tarzan's forest

B y looking at the rings of a tree stump, one can see what the weather has been like over the years, since hot and humid weather means thicker rings. What else do these rings tell us?

the tree's height ●

the tree's age ■

the forest's size ▲

A microclimate is a climate specific to a very small area and which depends on local factors. A forest can affect local climate by adding:

heat ●

humidity ■

sand ▲

T he sun's rays can be dangerous due to the ultraviolet (UV) radiation they contain. The gas found in the atmosphere which protects the earth from this radiation is:

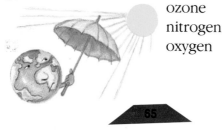

ozone ●

nitrogen ■

oxygen ▲

I n painting and sculpture, winter is often represented as an old man crowned with dried branches and holding dried fruits in his hand. Which tree stays green in the winter?

pine ●

oak ■

chestnut ▲

The atmosphere's gases let the earth store the heat that it both receives and emits. This process is called the greenhouse effect. A greenhouse is used for:

animals   ●

minerals   ■

plants   ▲

The monsoon is a very violent wind that brings torrential rains with it. In many Asian countries, there is so much water during monsoon season that everything grows very fast. People take advantage of this to plant:

cabbage   ●

rice   ■

pasta   ▲

The disappearance of dinosaurs may be explained by a sudden change in the earth's weather about 65 million years ago. According to one hypothesis, this change was due to a huge dust cloud that covered the earth after the fall of:

the moon ●

a meteorite ■

the sun ▲

C louds don't always disappear after dropping their rain. Their encounter with dry air changes them into:

water vapor
crumbs
light

"Thermic spread" is the average of the temperatures of the coldest and hottest months. It can be quite large in countries with hot summers and cold winters, like Russia or Canada. Where is this thermic spread small?

in the mountains
at sea
at the equator

71

S ummer is the time of great heat, when the sun shines at its brightest. Summer days:

get longer ●
get shorter ■
stay the same length ▲

72

T he hottest region of the globe is found in Ethiopia. The average yearly temperature is over 95°F (34°C). There are no clouds in the sky there because:

the sea is too far away ●
the ground is too hot ■
there is too much sand ▲

Vegetation depends on climate. When it rains a lot, grasses and plants grow abundantly. In hot deserts, vegetation is quite rare. In the American deserts, one can find:

cacti ●

firs ■

lianas ▲

Great climatic variations are measured over thousands of years. Despite the actual heating up of the atmosphere, scientists believe that in the next few thousand years:

there will be colder weather ●

the earth will disappear ■

the polar ice will melt ▲

When the weather is nice, the sky is blue. This is due to the diffusion of sunlight in the atmosphere. If this diffusion did not exist, the sky would appear:

white ●
black ■
yellow ▲

Clouds are generally associated with bad weather. Cumulonimbi are big black clouds that bring about

hurricanes ●
typhoons ■
thunderstorms ▲

I n ancient mythology, spring is often
represented as a young winged woman.
What is this woman's name?

Fauna ●
Laura ■
Flora ▲

Magnificent light phenomena with beautiful colors sometimes occur at the North (boreal) and South (austral) poles. These are:

auroras
eclipses
ellipses

The direction of the wind indicates its origin. When one speaks of a western wind, one means that it comes from the west. The tool that helps determine the wind's source is called a:

hygrometer
weather vane
anemometer

During autumn and winter, the air is often humid because it is loaded with a colorless and transparent gas which is actually:

water vapor ●

carbonic gas ■

chlorophyll ▲

The speed (or strength) of the wind at ground level is measured by the 12 degrees on Beaufort's scale, which classifies winds ranging from ½ mph (1 km/hr) to over 75 mph (120 km/hr). The strongest wind is called a:

storm ●

hurricane ■

gust ▲

S ome winds are characteristic to a region and thus have specific names. The coastal winds of North Africa are known as:

trade winds
zephyrs
siroccos

E very autumn, some birds migrate from North America to South America. Which of these birds do so?

pigeons
geese
robins

One can guess how far from a thunder-storm one is by measuring the time span between the lightning bolt and the thunder and multiplying that period by the speed of sound, which is:

30m/sec (10 ft/sec)

300m/sec (100 ft/sec) ■

1000m/sec (333 ft/sec) ▲

Fog can come about when hot and humid air meets the cold ground. Saying that fog descends is an error, since, in fact, it rises from the ground. It disappears due to:

rain

lower temperatures ■

solar heating ▲

Ice can assume different forms depending on where it is. What is the name of ice that falls from the sky?

hail
hologram
frost

In mythology, summer is often represented as a woman crowned by ripe sheaves of wheat. In her hands she usually holds:

a sickle
a hammer
a saw

Snow falls when the air temperature is around 32°F (0°C). Snow crystals have different shapes, but they're always hexagonal, which means that they have:

8 sides
6 sides
5 sides.

Wind direction is influenced by the earth's rotation. This rotation changes the winds' course, especially in the middle latitudes. Which physicist "discovered" this phenomenon?

Newton (1642–1727)
Coriolis (1792–1843)
Einstein (1879–1955)

Winds blow from high-pressure areas to low-pressure areas. The greater the difference in pressure between the two areas, the harder the winds blow. What is a trade wind?

a terrestrial wind ●
a fine rain ■
a marine wind ▲

Meteorology is the science that describes atmospheric phenomena. Regular measures and predictions have been made since the 18th century. Who created meteorology?

Aristotle ●
Plato ■
Galileo ▲

C hristmas marks the beginning of winter. Which holiday marks the beginning of spring?

Mother's Day   ●
Easter   ■
Father's Day   ▲

I n a single region, temperatures vary not only with the seasons, but also within a single day. The lowest temperature of the day is right after:

midnight   ●
sunset   ■
sunrise   ▲

C irrus are high clouds that look like long white flaments. They are made of ice crystals at −40°F/C. Their accumulation announces:

rain
snow
frost

T he first hygrometer (for measuring air humidity) made use of the fact that some materials lengthen when air is humid, and shrink when air is dry. This is true of:

hair
string
wire

M eteorological predictions are much more precise now that satellites are used for this purpose. They regularly beam back pictures of the earth and clouds. The first satellite, which blasted off in 1957, was named

Challenger ●

Sputnik ■

Ariane ▲

S ome illnesses are linked to the seasons. The flu is most prevalent during the winter, around January and February in the Northern Hemisphere. During the spring, the greatest risk is catching measles and:

whooping cough ●

a cold ■

chicken pox ▲

Wind erodes. Like water, it wears down rocks and sculpts the landscape. In the desert, it determines the shape of sand piles known as:

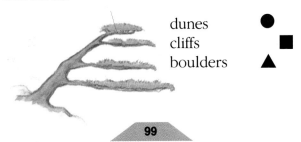

dunes ●

cliffs ■

boulders ▲

In Greek mythology, turbulent winds were locked into caves. Their master alone could liberate them. His name was:

Aeolus ●

Boreas ■

Zephyrus ▲

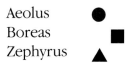

Fruits and vegetables don't all grow at the same time. Some are harvested in the summer, others during the fall. The carrot is sown at every season, depending on the variety. This is also true of:

buckwheat
potatoes
cabbage

Wind: Beaufort Scale

Force	Speed (in mph)	Description	Indicator
0	>1	calm	smoke goes straight up
1	1–3	light air	smoke shows wind direction
2	4–7	light breeze	one can feel the wind on one's face
3	8–12	gentle breeze	flags float
4	13–18	moderate breeze	sand flies
5	19–24	fresh breeze	branches move
6	25–31	strong breeze	electric wires whistle
7	32–38	moderate gale	it is hard to walk against the wind
8	39–46	fresh gale	it becomes
9	47–54	strong gale	impossible to walk against the wind
10	55–63	storm	children under
11	64–72	violent storm	12 years of age
12 to 16	73–136	hurricane	may be borne away.